We have always been coming to this morning

*For Rich Wyatt,
the better craftsman*

To the memory of Bill Farmer

*And always,
Debbie*

We have always been coming to this morning

Poems by Greg Kosmicki

ζ

Sandhills Press
Lewiston, Idaho / Grand Island, Nebraska

Also by Greg Kosmicki

when there wasn't any war, The Backwaters Press, 1987
How Things Happen, bradypress, 1997
nobody lives here who saw this sky, Missing Spoke Press, 1998
For My Son in a Motel Room, Sandhills Press, 1999
tables, chairs, wall, window, Sandhills Press, 2000
Greg Kosmicki: Greatest Hits, 1975-2000, Puddinghouse Press, 2001
The Patron Saint of Lost and Found, Lone Willow Press, 2003
Some Hero of the Past, Word Press, 2006

Copyright © 2007 Greg Kosmicki.

Cover art by Jaime Lee Hackbart
Copyright © 2007 Jaime Lee Hackbart

No part of this text may be copied or otherwise reprinted except in brief quotations for reviews.

Published by:	Sandhills Press
	Mark Sanders, Editor
	1437 Burrell Ave
	Lewiston, ID 83501

ISBN:	0-911015-57-4
	978-0-911015-57-7

Book design and layout by Mark Sanders.

Acknowledgments

Thanks to the editors of the journals and publications where some of these poems first appeared, some in different versions:

American Jones Building and Maintenance: "Packing," "Mailing Out Poems in Benson," and "Social Work."
The Greenfield Review: "A Short History of Western Civilization."
Least Loved Creature of the Really *Wild West* (Native West Press): "Why I Watch Sparrows."
Many Voices, One Song: "Ordinary Time."
Nebraska Poets Calendar: "Thoughts of the Encounter."
New Letters: "The Solution."
Pebble: "The Sparrows."
Plainsongs: "Roadhunting, 1972."
Rag Mag: "Nap."
The Temple: "Sitting in the car in front of a 7-11."
The Windless Orchard: "Skunk Beer."
Whole Notes: "the usefulness of vacant lots."

"Oh, Johnny, Oh!" and "A Short History of Western Civilization," appeared in *Poets Against the War,* online version.

A slightly different version of "Sacrifice" was published in *Bison Poems: Of Bison and the Great Plains,* T. G. Franti, Editor, Center for Great Plains Studies, University of Nebraska-Lincoln, 2002

"Social Work", "Mailing Out Poems In Benson", and "Relationship" were published as part of a Feature Poet section in *Pudding #40.*

"The Stuff that Didn't Get Into the Report", "A Short History of Western Civilization", "A Certain Poor Coffee Farmer", "The Solution", "Eating Supper, Watching the News", "My Flag", and "History" were part of a chapbook, *when there wasn't any war,* from The Backwaters Press, 1988.

I would also like to thank Jonathan Holden for his very close reading of this manuscript, and for his numerous comments and suggestions.

Table of Contents

1. The Stuff that Didn't Get into the Report

A Short History of Western Civilization / 11
The Stuff that Didn't Get into the Report / 12
A Certain Poor Coffee Farmer / 13
The Solution / 14
Eating Supper, Watching the News / 15
My Flag / 16
History / 18
The Sparrows / 19
The Wind / 20
I awaken in a group home for the mentally handicapped / 27
the usefulness of vacant lots / 28
Migration / 29
Pissing at the Wonder Bar, 1969 / 32

2. Because They Have Witnessed Everything

After Love / 37
The Dandelion / 38
Relationship / 40
Agent Orange / 41
4/17/94 / 43
Earth Day Inventory / 51
Why I Watch Sparrows / 55
Sitting in the car in front of a 7-11 / 58
7-8-94 / 61
Social Work / 63
Roadhunting, 1972 / 65
Packing / 66

3. Poem an Old Drunk Street Poet Told My Son

Poem an Old Drunk Street Poet Told My Son at The Greyhound Station / 75
Mailing Out Poems in Benson / 76
Audrey / 78
Looking for my daughter / 79
Thoughts of the Encounter / 80
The Candle / 82
The Museum of the Fur Trade, Chadron, Nebraska / 83
Tomorrow at Seven / 84
Skunk Beer / 86
Nap / 87
It is only 4 AM / 89
Oh, Johnny, Oh! / 90
Ordinary Time / 91
Cricket / 93
Sacrifice / 95
Peanut Butter / 96
Cricket Redux / 98
The Microwave / 99
Front Page Story in the *Omaha World-Herald* / 100
Doing Laundry / 102
To the Citizens of Omaha, Nebraska / 104
This Morning / 105
What I Like / 106

About the Author / 108

1. The Stuff that Didn't Get into The Report

> *"...how many times can a man turn his head and pretend that he just doesn't see..."*
>
> Bob Dylan
> "Blowin' in the Wind"

A Short History of Western Civilization

First the good guys beat the bad guys.
Then the bad guys beat the good guys.
But the good guys were strong, they had God
on their side, they rose up
and beat the bad guys.
Then the bad guys beat the good guys.
Then most people left over got smallpox.
Then the good guys beat the bad guys.
Many people starved during this.
Then the bad guys rose up, they had
God on their side, they were strong,
they beat the good guys.
But the good guys had God too
so they beat the bad guys.
Then half the people left over died of plague.
The bad guys wouldn't learn.
They beat the good guys again.
Then the good guys beat the bad guys.
The people who remained starved.
Then the bad guys beat the good guys.
Then the good guys got the upper hand
and stomped the bad guys.
Then the people left over died of famine.
Then it was yesterday.
Then it was tomorrow.

The Stuff that Didn't Get into the Report

He was a minute late so was docked an hour.
She stood in line so long and then the window closed.
The cigarette machine at Cy's gypped him of 95¢.
A pretty girl in a blue dress walked in and sat down.
The president of the company ordered up a ham on rye.
Just after the final buzzer a sparrow lighted on a branch by the east
    window.
He had never believed in omens but liked the Norwegian penny he found.
The machines break down the body as well as themselves she screamed.

A Certain Poor Coffee Farmer

A certain poor coffee farmer who lived in a certain poor country in South America one day was out picking his few coffee beans for the day when an American television crew came piling into the front yard of his humble brick and tin house. All six of his chickens scattered to the far corners of the yard, his wife stopped pumping water at the well, and the children ran over to her and hid behind her skirts. The TV crew jumped out of the truck and the director began shouting directions. Soon the portable generator was cranking out thousands of volts of electricity a second, more than the farmer would use in his lifetime if a rural electrification program were started today by his country, which wasn't likely, and the bright lights the television crew had set up made the farmer start to sweat. The crew rushed around and filmed as many cassettes of stuff as they could: the groves, the mountains, the picturesque hut. Then they chop-chop packed their gear back into their trucks and a helicopter plopped out of the sky into the yard, scaring the pig as well as the chickens and the farmer and his family, and flew off with the director. Then the prop men folded up the fences and the hut and disassembled the bushes and the yard. They tried to fold up the farmer and his family but they wouldn't fold.

The Solution

Hundreds of people ran out into the streets
they were so sad, they were so tired of war
and when there wasn't any war
they were so tired of peace
they were sticking knives in their eyes
and rubbing hot coals in their ears
their children were running along behind them
but they didn't care
about their children
they wanted to give up
they had done enough
they thought
they didn't care if they lived or not
with such suffering who
can stand to be alive
the children can fend for themselves
they'll just grow into
a life of torture
like ours we can't stand it
any longer why should it be us
take our children they screamed
shoving their children in front
take them take them take them

Eating Supper, Watching the News

Grandfather, one of the old and young
left behind, in his loose white
peasant's shirt and gray hat

must run, gun slung at shoulder
down the hill toward the camera,
away from the thick white walls
that are home, the young ones at hand.

And it is not as if we don't sense
the tearing sadness of this act
as we slice half-raw steaks
and rest our forks among the peas.

Reducing his life's most important actions
to the representational,
TV cameras watch only him
while the brutal scene
repeats itself in every doorway
of this distant village,

where the old run,
clutching all that is left to them,

the young, who are crying.

My Flag

It is after dinner and I go to shake
the crumbs from the tablecloth.
They fall down onto the porch steps

for the crickets and the mice and ants.
We live in a great country,
there is enough for all.

The tablecloth unfurls lightly on the held breath
of the still fall night air
and it seems to me to be like a flag

with the blue stripe all around the border
and the blue stripe enclosing the field at center,
a field that encloses some flowers

but could not hold in even all the flowers
since some of them have escaped
and drifted, as on water or a breeze

toward the bright blue border.
It is the flag of the friendly country,
where even the vermin have enough to eat,

and I'm waving it from my porch for everyone.
I want you to come and join me
and my family, I want you to sit

at my table and have bread and lasagna with us
so we can talk about the war and the taxes,
I want you to help me shake crumbs on the porch,

I want to wash it and iron it and fold it safely,
to place it gently and with respect in the drawer
for our next dinner when we will not have

marched under any other flag
for I know you could not be a traitor to me.
We will all be so insanely happy

we had not yet had to die for any cause.
I want you to spill your wine.
I want you to get bread crumbs on my flag.

History

A secret the badger knows the ants do not.
But what the ants can tell is important to understand.

Sometimes a bird will come to sit, on a windowsill, unbidden.
In china-thin bones are stored many messages.

You have seen it—a flower growing, a pretty yellow one, in sludge.
You have been witness to many rainbows.

Under a tree, in stiff brown grass, we said we had love.
While spiders, fulfilling an ancient demand, spun nets in abandoned
    corners.

The raffle tree shook out tickets, which were leaves.
In the quiet of a perpetual evening we went into our houses.

On an open plain, a few dry buttes in the distance, deer lifted their heads,
    a moment.
Three short hymns were stuck together with cellophane tape,
    then we sang.

The sadness of the board fence became evident by morning.
But many lunches were packed and hearts filled with desire.

Malicious intent, the old standby, was once again given center stage.
Old people in donated coats cut small pieces of cheese.

The President went once more to bed, a vast loneliness he could not
    understand.
A rusted nail lay between two gravel pieces on the county road.

Erosion had finally worn down everything, so a new monument was
    planned.
A sparrow sat in a leafless tree and did not sing.

The Sparrows

The sparrows in winter have a tough time. The food supply diminishes, then dries up altogether. People feed them, then go away on vacation. Snow comes, the seeds are all covered. The sparrows flock together all day long and go to the places that they know there will be seed. They must eat their own body weight every day to survive. They drip down out of the branches to feed. They flash back up at a sound. They wait, they cock their heads, they stay nervous and wary. They talk among themselves. They look for danger. They fly up into the higher trees. They come cautiously back to the bushes. The old man has died, but they do not know it.

The Wind

1.
I stood in that pasture of virgin sod
wrapped in the wind
clumps of buffalo grass ancient as earth
growing out of limestone soil
made of bones and plants and shells

She spoke to me
she told me my name but I could not understand

Already as a child I was lost
and could not decipher even the simplest meanings
from the movement of grasses

I ran to her, I cried out like a man in agony
I stumbled and fell on the hard rock
I tasted dust in my mouth
cactus spines pierced through my shirt

I saw a beetle in the chalk dust in front of me—
this was my brother but I did not know him

2.
This is what the Boatswain's Mate said:
"They might send women and children
in front of them.
They might send little old ladies,
but you knock 'em down, Sailors,
cuz if you don't I'll be right behind you
and I'll fuck you up bad."

On a great lake of my country I had come

to keep the peace.
I was 20 years old.

The body found frozen at the shore,
word had it, was a narc's. A fitting death.

We walked out among the waters on the jetty
made of building waste, my present girl and I.

The wind a wounded beast's death howl—

I could not understand the music or the girl,
myself, or my country,
the water, or the wind.

3.
Why could I never understand what my shoes
were screaming at me?
How could I have possibly misunderstood
the language of the bathroom sink
the low animal sighings of the refrigerator,
the incessant chatter of the marigolds,
the somber attitudes of cucumbers?
What could I have impossibly been dreaming of?
How could I have had a dream
who couldn't read the book of an ordinary day,
who did not know the lexicon of the wind
each moment as he was living and dying in it?

4.
I did it! I did it! I held her down
and heard her low sobbing beneath me.
Where the 72 steps went down to the water

we had walked that afternoon
among the golden leaves,
out past the concrete structure
to where the alewives washed up on the shore
and signs warned us not to swim or drink.
We made a fire, out of someone else's leavings,
drank cheap fruit wine and smoked Moroccan hash.
She told me all her father
and brothers had done to her.
Her honesty meant nothing to me.
She moaned and sobbed and asked me not to.

Years later in a violent windstorm
when I was out of control of my truck
and almost lost I realized,
I, too,
had become one of the rapists.

5.
At the head of the stairs I stood
and growled,
a drunken, happy bear.
I had become Mark's father by then.
Even as I fell and hurt my shoulder
he ran outside into the rain.
I followed him where he ran,
the rain washing down into my face and eyes.
We came back, laughing, covered with alley mud:
We had been pelted with the wind and the rain,
we had covered ourselves with soil of the earth,
we were primeval, mud creatures.
Something broke inside of me that day
and started to seep out slowly
and I knew that this boy and I would love each other forever.

6.
Wineheart's chick we were all going to ball
was sloppy overweight, blonde bleached,
dressed like a hippie,
had a fringed vest and everything,
and a red beat-up convertible.
We got over to her place and the tub
was filled with green shit
because the toilet backed up
so she and her kids
had been using the tub.
Trash in bags was piled 3-feet deep
by the fridge.

Before anything, we decided we'd better get back to the base.
Somebody came up with an excuse and borrowed her car.
We stopped in for some smokes.
I almost gouged out Roy "The Boy's" eyes
because he harassed me by pulling off my glasses.
He taunted me and wouldn't give them back.
For weeks afterwards his eyes hurt him.

It had been a hot, dry day, no wind
but night had changed to cold.
We sat in the car and waited.

7.
My father kicks my bike across the garage floor.

Though I did not leave it there
his anger kicks me.

Outside, tan on blue, a summer dust storm.

A small boy, big black glasses,
one of my friends called me "Frog Eyes."

I never understood that kick
until years later my father's anger became my own.

8.
By wing, airless, soundless, windless, wordless, dry,
I came to the place where I got out of the plane
with others of my kind
and a man screamed at us
to get our fucking toes on the curb and keep them there.
I had a hard time not laughing.

Next morning we awoke to a trash can
drummed on by a man with a shaven head named Lulow
who had got there three days before us
and already was a reject.

Less than 5 weeks later I choked a man
because he laughed in formation
outside the mess hall.

I didn't know it then
but I had just made it my war.

9.
I loved her so much
but it was a feeling
I didn't understand.
I ran outside with all my clothes off
and hugged her.
Years later, during a heavy rain
the wind twisted her and split her in two.

10.
Down the 72 steps to the dead alewives, the poison lake,
Gallo Spanada and hash.

I lay on the pebbles like a dead man,
rain pouring in my open eyes and mouth.
The other guys were back in the trees
laughing and smoking.
On the portable, War sang "Spill wine, get that girl."

There was nothing else for me.

11.
Every summer Mom drove us the sixty miles
on the twisty road south of town through the Sandhills
to the town named after a man
thrown out of a wagon to die
by his fellow pilgrims.
Dr. Gridley put drops in our eyes.
Then we waited in this room like corpses,
then we sat in a chair,
then we got these funny square brown sunglasses.
Distorted through the lenses of those afternoons,
out into blinding sunlight,
into dry wind-blown sand,
we crept, survivors at our mother's hand.

12.
There was a job listed in the paper.
I was sitting across from a man behind a desk
in an insurance office
in Lincoln, Nebraska,
across the highway from the State Pen.

Coming here the wind had just about blown the V-Dub off the road.

I was doing my best to convince him to hire me.
I had even gotten a haircut.
I didn't tell him
I hated America
I hated armies
I hated the flag
I hated businessmen
I hated insurance
and I left my one suit
in California.

To impress them I borrowed a sports jacket from a friend.
The jacket had been in storage for years.

The insurance man got up to talk to someone
and left the room.

He seemed nervous.
I think he thought I was going to kill him.

I looked down at my lapel.
A giant wood cockroach was sitting on it.

I knew I had been saved.

I awaken in a group home for the mentally handicapped

I lived inside a woman—
when I came out, it was a different world.

Although I knew nothing about it
the Chinese had not yet invaded Korea.
We didn't even have the hula hoop.

I grew cold in that room and I cried.
Before that I had known only warmth
a few muffled voices, bowel sounds
like whale song,
the quiet rhythm of my one home's heart.

*

When I awoke I was 40.
I had a wife and two kids
six payments left
on a broken car
and a job in a group home.

A mentally handicapped man
was screaming obscenities in my face.

Snow was coming down outside.

I blinked my eyes and saw he was Christ.
He threw himself on the floor.
He refused to get up.

the usefulness of vacant lots

Open places where my spirit unfurls with the leaves of weeds
they place a measurable distance around someone's future.

Understandable stretches of ground not like the Himalayas
provide useful lines around which trees can grow.

Final resting place for the luckless dismembered plastic doll
bit of brick, shard of glass, length of wire,

speak to us of the joy of leaving things unfinished.

Summer jungle for our patchwork-quilt cat Snuggles
where some trillion to the googleplex power of insects

charge out with massive chitinous pincers
or sip quietly the life-juice of weeds.

Hothouse of slime-molds, fungi, moss and lichens
place where sunlight does its best work,

last finger holds of the dying atmosphere.

Migration

"See Dad there they are! There's some more of those birds!"
"Ah, yes! The geese! I thought it was the geese
you saw last night!"
It must have been like a vision to her—

have you ever seen them, flying at night over a city,
bellies lit from the glare of lamps
a surreal procession of distracted birds
looking for a place to land
where community memory must tell them
Here is our place to land
Here is where the fathers and mothers slept and fed?
But it is night, they are tired
there are no marshes, no bogs
no fields full of grain leavings, no water
but only flat concrete parking lots
housetops, rows of lights,
some flicking on and off,
car tops, flat roofs, sloped roofs, angled roofs
no place to land, so they stay
they stay where they can stay no longer
like tired moths beating their wings
against the memory of a flame at a dead lightbulb,
they cannot land, they can't come to rest
and my daughter has seen them
as an apparition, a sighting, a seeing.

We saw the geese again this early fall morning
and she says
"See they're flying in that shape!
See that, Dad!"
I read somewhere once about the mechanics of the "V,"
how the lead goose takes the brunt of the wind

works hardest in cutting a hole into the air
the others magically pass through,
flies in this position for a while
maybe 15 or 20 minutes
then drops back and another
takes over so the other geese work less
but still get to come along,
that eventually perhaps several others will take the lead.

I tell her all this stuff
and she listens politely as she always does
she knows I tend to ramble
and then I start to tell her about the bison
in the snowstorms but she changes the subject
gently guiding me like the lead goose.

Just before we turned off the highway
towards the school building where I took her
so that some other members of our species might lead her
I remembered a moment some years ago
as I drove across the Sandhills of Western Nebraska
but I didn't tell her.
She was already talking about something else
some little girl topic, her curiosity about the geese
fulfilled miles ago by my earnest bombast
but I was stuck on migration

and I thought of that rain-swept afternoon
in my UPS package car
as I whipped across the ancient Sandhills—
these dunes of sand
stopped in mid-storm, mid-sentence almost,

when I saw the pelicans with their gangly necks
pursuing their strange preoccupation with being birds

when they obviously have not been designed for it
with rain slicker beaks and driftwood chunk-shaped bodies.

I slowed down my brown van
almost to a stop and somewhere the dust
I had disarranged in my haste in passing fell behind me
into a neat pattern onto the blacktop.
I watched as the pelicans flew.

Their flight as a flock one continuous integrated movement—
the lead pelican pumps its wings three times,
rises to a peak,
the tip of a swell,
then does not pump,
slowly drops down.
The one behind the leader pumps
three times,
rises up to the peak,
then slowly drifts down.

This motion repeated
the length of the flock
so that you will witness pelicans' flight
as a stunning wave-like motion,
each bird so ungainly
that when you think exactly
there is no hope,
the bird must crash down
it can't possibly pull itself out of this one,

it pumps its wings again to follow up the wave
made by the one in front of it,
each bird
rolling up to the crest
and down through the trough
of this sacred living together on earth.

Pissing at the Wonder Bar, 1969

in my hometown looking at
piss all over the floor
dumb shithouse writings on the wall
when this big Indian guy comes in
tries to start a fight.

Wasted more than I was
who'd been drinking five or six hours
as was the custom
weekends in Alliance, Nebraska,
whatever it was about, he forgot,

starts to talk,
wants to know
did I want to get it on
with his sister?

I who
for years
had gotten
nothing on

lie *No man I already got it
two times tonight*

he says
Whoa! Two times! No shit!

slaps me on the back

says Red Cloud
was his great-great-uncle

I believe him—
what's the point in lying?

Stale piss, dark smoke,
faces, beer lights,

laughter
by sunrise
no one of us
would remember
the reason for.

2. Because They Have Witnessed Everything

After Love

How good it is to lie here in dark to hear sounds through the open
    window
second day of March in the year of Nineteen-Hundred-and-Ninety-Two
    in a warm spell
sound of dogs barking, an occasional car passing
hearing your breathing, feeling the warmth of your body, talking low,

to get up, go into the dark hallway like a shadow to hear
our ten-year-old daughter talk and to discover it is not in her sleep
because she asks us, ever so politely,
to keep our voices down because she is trying to sleep.

The Dandelion

I want to go to bed
but before I do
I want to write a poem
about the dandelion by my back door
because I saw the dandelion
when I came out one morning this week
to go to work and ever since then
I've wanted to write a poem
it was so yellow.
It is so tough the only way you can get rid of it
is to poison it heavily
or to get a shovel and dig it out
since it has that tremendous taproot.
It's really rooted in this place!
It goes down deep into the earth
and it intends to stay where it is
and you can hack it off
do a poor job of killing
and it'll be back
like one of those B-movie creatures.
It's here to stay, man! It's got an attitude!
You've got to murder it
and murder it good.
It's tougher than a domestic flower but just as beautiful.
A whole field full of them isn't less pleasing
to the eye than a field of tulips.
I think maybe it's their commonness that gets me
more than anything, which is what also
drives lawn owners wild too and is probably
why people despise them. But I tell you,
I looked until I found a woman to marry
who loved dandelions as much as I do.

Of the blossoms, too, I want to sing
because yellow is the best color in the world,
because the dandelion has the color yellow
on its mind most all the time, because yellow
is all good things
like corn and sun and yellow paint,
because egg yolks are yellow
and pacifists are yellow
and wimps like the yellow-bellied cowards in the cowboy movies.
When one yellow honey-flavored head wilts away
after its day or two of glory another one
equally fine appears, a sort of trashable mutable art
of replaceable expendable color,
the color that drove Van Gogh crazy
by its sheer power to attract light
the way the sun attracts a planet maybe
or the whole wacky universe
attracts life so that we all sprang up.

Braced on translucent straws of juice in thrall with turgor
the color is there to vigorously proclaim
the victory of the color yellow over everything,
even the stupidity of homeowners,
who years ago in less exalted times
would eat those humble serrated leaves
more beautiful and heart-breaking in their perfection
than the tallest spruce,
more clean in their lines
than the most carefully chipped obsidian spearheads.
Endurance, productivity, beauty, rootedness,
perfection of form, outrageous color expressivity,
these hated enemies of all lawn-keepers possess
not one character flaw except the misfortune
of being members of an outcast group of plants
we call the weeds.

relationship

1.
Anything I write down
about sparrows has been written down

by others, in pure scientific language
and in the other languages

but they still are out there looking for grain
and love.

2.
Even though I have thought about them,
also written about them, some,
it has affected their lives little.

How I did affect their lives
was by putting out a mixture of milo,
cracked corn,

wheat and sunflower seeds
and by making sure
it is always there.

3.
Once I started to put the seed out
even over the objections
because of expense
of my wife

she also
came to love seeing them
each day at a certain time
so that her life too was changed.

Agent Orange

for Clyde Gillespie

You come back with a broken fist
by medevac from the bush to Clean Ortho—3-East.
I'm stationed on 3-West, Dirty Ortho,
cleaning and debriding wounds. Corpsman says,
"A grunt on Three-E says he's from your hometown."

I come over on break-time.
You're there two days, then booted out,
a euphemistic "less-than-honorable" discharge
in a less-than-honorable war.
We never got together like we said.

One time at college a couple years before
though you barely knew me you took care of me
drunk slobbering about my dead brother.
Last thing I heard you were back in our hometown
dead of cancer at 27
but hell you know that's not true.

Last night you were with me again
after poetry and beer
still had your crew-cut brown hair
and as you spoke I remembered your gentleness
that night I was wasted and broken
drinking buddies sick of my wailing

heard your husky smoke voice as you retold
the story from the 3-East ward
how you broke your fist,
cold-cocking that Zero in Nam

showed me again the right uppercut
that did it got you that white cast
and the discharge. Saw again
your Jesus Christ brown eyes.

4/17/94

(I start out to write this
just past midnight
a day of record high heat
tail end of that day
the beginning, really, of the next)

in darkness

        where a man wanders the streets
shouting obscenities at the dogs
which shout, in their own fashion
obscenities at him,
        I can hear him
as he heads south on 36th
out of the range of hearing
        hear him as he comes back
somewhere close by
my neighbor's dogs going crazy for 20 minutes

        he shouting back at them,
                at God
at the system
                at his life—

    Last night, it was the same thing

I'm a citizen
        I have to decide:
call him in
to the cops
        as a disturber of the
peace,
                or let it ride

call tomorrow if he's out again—

Earlier this afternoon I heard
                              two shots
                                        while Briana and I
sat on the front porch after
shucking corn

Sitting in a lawn chair
                    I was reading a book
of Chinese poetry

                she had a big illustrated
Mother Goose she quoted from
            the ones she knew by heart
had me read
            to her the ones
she didn't know

There are so many!

(I remember my suspicions
of questionable origins
of the little black hen story
                        how she lays eggs just
for gentlemen)

think how these rhymes
have come down
intact and meaningless
                    for 20th Century
                city dwellers
for the most part
            but for the music
of the language

We go in for supper
        spaghetti, corn on the cob

Grandma's here today from San Diego
        just flown in a couple hours ago

Eat, clean up, do the nightly
necessary rituals,
        some of the family
                parks in front of the TV
I take my book and read
after bringing up a load of laundry

Tired Briana pushes
        about 20 of Debbie's buttons
in the bath
        so I take over
        get her bathed

Near the end of her bath
she pulls down all the towels

into the tub
for a joke

One of the two of us
in the bathroom
is angry

but the other one doesn't
recognize that

I get her out after
rinsing her hair
with fresh water from the tap

After-the-bath ritual begins
we skip tonight the usual book
she's tired enough she doesn't care
then snack (apple, cored and sliced), various
meddies (tonight: Robitussin
for the cough, cortizone for the
incipient exzema)
                          kiss Grandma   Mom and Audrey
all mesmerized by the TV movie
                upstairs then to tuck, sing
and pray
                Without this, it's no go
most often,   tonight
                she's conked out in the middle
                                        of prayers
Into the hallway
        to meditate
against the noise of the TV voices

        fruitless,
no quiet,
        go back down
bring the load up from the washer
                to the bedroom (Debbie's wet
sweatshirts to dry
    on hangers)
           go back down
to the basement   get the snake
                              go back up
struggle
in the bathtub 20 minutes
                with lost hair and slime

It runs free

          Clean the tub

Back downstairs to put
               the snake away

Read Chinese poetry a while
                    (too long—didn't leave
                    enough time for exercise)

get on the exercise bike for ten minutes
                           at ten 'til ten

          leave at ten to get
     Mark from work

On the way back
            we hear   five or six
shots,
      from somewhere
                      in the direction of our house

At home,
       Debbie says   she too   heard them

         Mark goes to bed
after reading
      about Kurt Cobain's death
              in *People*

Grandma finally adjusted
       (her shingles hurt her)
lays herself down to sleep on the couch

Upstairs I bathe
wash off hair clippings

                        from my haircut today

    start this
                                        somebody
    a block or two away
                                                starts to honk
    their car horn relentlessly,
                                stops
            starts up again

    Ambulances keer through streets
                                        fire engines, police wail
    private vehicles boom by
    bass rattles our windows

    Whatever's going on out there
    dogs   somewhere
    bark at it:

    This is what a poet can do—
    or one kind of poet,
    or one poet

    chronicle the days
    when the sun came out
    as it did today and got
    hot, or when it doesn't,
            chronicle
    the life of one family
                    chronicle   the birds
    at the feeding places
    (mostly grackles and blackbirds today

                and underneath this sheet a flock
                                    of letter A's

drawn last August by Briana

                    slipping like a string
     of blackbirds
                                                through the
sky
)

chronicle these days
                  how things
make sense,
       or seem to
or don't make any sense at all

chronicle how by writing
                 them all down anyway
they all make sense
         somehow—

        If we don't
leave a trail
                (like going into the deep
dark forest trailing
       our track of crumbs)

who can follow?

Who might wind up in the oven?

Who else
                     will write
the rhyme
     for the children
about

                        the Black Prince
who screams
                his agony
                                in the streets outside my house?

Earth Day Inventory

For today's accounting: no gunshots yet—
3 places where blisters
will be raised up on the palm of my right hand,
one minor scratch.

One vision of Briana sitting at the altar railing
before Mass, the breeze
from the open side door
lifting up her hair to blow
so gently around her radiant face.

50 seeds of corn planted, more or less
in 2 straight lines of 10 holes
dug through the sod,
ten pieces of sod transplanted
in last year's failed garden.

One son transported to work
picked up again at ten
one daughter taken to a friend's
at 3, after 15 minutes
extra driving through traffic
stalled on 80 because of a crash
between two cars.

We saw 75 acres of dreams
the new Botanical Gardens
visited the advertised
6,000 tulips, which we doubted.
Audrey joked she was so thrilled
she should have brought her movie camera
and then one guy in front of us
was videotaping the tulips!

We got lost once, looking
for the gardens.
We took one wrong turn from the start
then 4 others, gave up
finally, after wading through the traffic by Rosenblatt
asked for directions at the traveler's information booth
drove there straight away.
He said we're not the first
to ask the way today
handed me a pre-written slip.
He said right now you have to have vision
to see the the 75 acres
as it will be in 10 years.
We discovered you also had to have vision
to see 6,000 tulips.
One friend of ours went along,
we stopped twice after the traffic jam
dropped off Audrey at her friend's
stopped by Hy-Vee on the way home,
and later Barb's to drop her off.
Debbie bought 4 cherry bagels
I wolfed down two
she the others. Barb had a single
bag of popcorn. Briana crushed a bag
filled with who knows how many
peanut M&M's
covered herself from head to toe
with chocolate. At Hy-Vee
I called Mark to get him up,
let the phone ring 40 times (I counted)
but it never roused him.
We hurried through the checkout
Barb with her six items
we with our three.

At ten I picked up Mark.
I stopped at the 7-11
to get 5 bucks on #4.
The guy took my check without a second glance.
I flipped the tank lid open
and there were the six rocks
Briana placed some time
beside the spout
in her game she plays.
I liked that, to see those rocks.
It's like she left her calling card
for me so I could see those rocks
and think of her and her zaniness.
I left them there, drove
to Hardee's and saw again
the moon, that biggest rock, almost full,
ten bazillion gallons,
which I had seen once before
tonight, when I pulled out
of the garage and thought
this must the the millionth time
I've seen her, the moon,
and the breath I'm taking
of this liquid air must be the trillionth—

this in all my one life
in which today I planted corn
ate three meals
loved one god
one family
used one spade, cross-cut saw
hand ax, hammer, car,
saw one moon,
wore two shirts
two pairs of pants

one pair of socks
a pair of boots and a pair of shoes
drank one-and-a-half cups of coffee
had one Slurpee and two snacks
shit twice, peed 6 times
talked to more than 40 people
not one of whom tried to harm me

Why I Watch Sparrows

because they are ordinary.
because they are everywhere.
because they have to scrabble each day for food.
because they are not flashy.
because they are intent on their business.
because they are adapted to their lives.
because they do nothing extraordinary.
because they get shoved about by squirrels.
because they are mentioned in the Bible.
because they depend on Earth.
because they stay for winter.
because they stay for summer.
because they make no shows.
because they look out for each other.
because they follow their rules.
because of their diminutive size.
because they make precise movements.
because they can land on a chain-link fence.
because they can land in a chain-link fence.
because they are mentioned in Zen koans.
because they can pick up a grain at a time with their beaks.
because they are always vigilant.
because they are not gaudy.
because they can peck at the ground without mashing their beaks.
because they can land on a stem of grass.
because they are always busy with something.
because they don't sit around and think about it.
because they live inside their lives.
because they appear to understand their lives.
because they are inscrutable to us.
because they are not inscrutable to themselves.
because they hop to walk.
because they give each other space.

because they form patterns when they peck at the grain.
because they learn to trust humans.
because they live around us.
because they are written about by Dr. Williams.
because my mother hates them.
because they have life.
because they hang together.
because they puff up their feathers in the cold.
because they remind me of water.
because I have to feed them.
because they are afraid of us.
because they jump up at a noise.
because they fly in patterns.
because they watch in patterns.
because of the precise movements of their heads.
because I shot one with a BB gun when I was a kid.
because I shot them with a .22 a few years later.
because ammunition companies make .22 shells called bird shot to kill them.
because the shells are crimped golden and beautiful.
because I never got any thrill out of killing them.
because many people consider them to be pests.
because they flew in the quonsets where the tractor was parked.
because they built their nests in the corners of the quonsets.
because their nest were built of twigs and bits of string.
because they fly up all at once.
because they are of one mind.
because they have a simple order.
because they have built no cities.
because they have worn no clothes.
because they have started no wars.
because they have out lived Caesar in all his robes.
because they have outlived Hitler in all his hate.
because they don't believe in politics.
because they keep focused on the real.

because they have no illusions.
because they are not trying to change the world.
because they fit in.
because they give back.
because they seem very stern but must be gentle in their hearts.
because I can guess all these things about them.
because they do not pay attention to me except when they are hungry.
because they are destined to be some of the last creatures.
because they think for themselves.
because so many other birds are gone from our lives.
because the frogs and toads are disappearing.
because they have not ceased to be.
because they live wrapped in the meanings of their lives.
because they have witnessed
everything.

Sitting in the car in front of a 7-11

Debbie and the kids gone in for a Slurpee
                                              in the middle
       of a long
                pleasure trip
on a hot day

              I watch a Mexican woman
              in a gray, loose, ill-fitting dress
talk on the telephone
about something urgent—
                          a place to live
                          a job
                          the next meal, money
for gas—
         while two small guys
         her kids, I guess,
                      run back and forth
    in front of me on the bubble gum-
                     and spit-covered sidewalk
happy, distracted, wild.

The man with her
                   seems the wrong age to be their father
                   too young to be grandpa
                   too old to be big brother

who like the woman
seems to have lived

        not forty years
        but
        generations
                  existing somehow out of time

while seriously in it.

                Four lives   one tableau
I'm witness to
                like one of the Mysteries
or an unrecorded occurrence from the Bible:
                                  The Phone Call in Omaha at the 7-ll.

Only she
                        and sorrow know
      what she will have to do.

He
              leans against a blue gray Chevy van faded
              the color of the washed-out jeans he wears
              worn out and re-worn out
              in an unfashionable life spent bent

                        hoeing someone else's potatoes and beans
                        picking grapes coated with poison
                        slicing pigs and fingers into pieces
                        hauling offal from slaughterhouses,

                        her desperate eyes glance across the space
                        of glass reflecting

                                  a swatch of blue
                                  a patch of Phillips 66
                                  my car and me

                  floating over

                                  bags of chips
                                  plastic cans of oil

                                        girlie mags—

he worries
            the boys
                    may run into trouble
    calls gently

                            niños, niños.

7-8-94

Up late at night to read smart-ass poems by smart-assed poets
in love with the sounds of their cuteness
and their syllables, I hear the screams
of children through my open kitchen window.
These are no metaphorical screams but screams for real.
There is no smart-ass poet lilting syllables about them.
Some child in the house behind my house
is getting beaten or otherwise abused.
This is my life after dark, after my family
has gone to bed, this is my muse.
Earlier, 10 *thug thug thugs* of semi-automatic fire,
some other kids outside laughing, more shots
down the street the other way, the squeal of tires.
Now the screaming child.

Unlike a month ago
when I called the cops to break up a row
some other neighbors were having,
both madly drunk
and screaming in the darkness,
he throwing her out,
she screaming and cursing 20 minutes straight at one,
and starting back up again at 3:30
when I called the cops,
then again at 5, and when I called the cops again
they came and found her
sitting on the corner on the curb and took her away—
unlike that one this
is just the voice of a child.

I go outside to get closer and listen: nothing.
The neighbor dogs bark on all sides
voices choking against their chains

but in the mercury vapor light behind our house
the scene is one of utter calmness
draped in leaves.

No more screaming from the house
so I go on back and stand a while by the garage
to look at the stars,
and listen, against my will
to the strangled voices of the dogs.

Straight up above me I see the star
the world seems to spin on,
then watch as Ursa Major, renamed
in our dorky American blandness, The Big Dipper,
silently pours out her starry load of darkness.

Social Work

I interview a guy only ten years older than me
who's had 24 strokes since 1989
whose heart is bad from it, diabetes complications,
who can't use his body for anything
a mass of flesh to store his brain
except for his left arm and hand
which he can use to type out messages
in the blue letters on the telephone device for the deaf:

I want to move. Help me. They took the money.

The whole time this woman
who lets him stay in her house
and takes care of him
and says she's his only friend
signals something to me behind his back
I can't quite understand—

He's crazy? He can't move? He's almost dead?

I can't tell.

He sits in the wheelchair in front of me, drools,
grimaces to try to make me understand.

She says he understands everything spoken
but after the first few strokes
his two sons had him declared incompetent
took all his money and two houses
then stuck him in a VA home.

She says they shoved him off in a corner there
changed him once a day.

Repeatedly he breaks out in an awful laugh he can't control
as I sit there on the couch facing him.

I want to cry out
he looks so much like my father.

Roadhunting, 1972

Yellow afternoon sunlight
flows on winter days across violet snow
through milky windows
of another of those beat-up old cars Dad is forever buying.

We smoke cigarettes and talk about how we've got to quit.
There are questions we don't ask—
What is it compels two men
father and brother of a dead man
to drive around by cornfields
with dangerous weapons, in bad weather
make small talk and smoke?

A pheasant leaps from the underbrush
a dazzling sacrifice of fear

we slam our doors open
pump shells into chambers

fire at the empty air

Packing

Now we are once again packing boxes
full of our stuff
less stuff than the last time
less than the time before that
less than the time before that one, too.

We actually reached our peak
of the pile of stuff
3 houses and 6 years ago
when I was UPS-ing and Debbie
was teaching school and the family,
all caught up in getting and spending,
was growing apart.

I quit my job at UPS
it was a good job
by all the standard yardsticks
pay was good, benefits too
hours long and hard but only
Monday through Friday—

it was like a divorce, really,
the kids crying that first night,
Mark especially, then Audrey came up
with her brave child's words
about new beginnings.

Debbie finished out the year
at school, we tried to sell the house
but couldn't, I worked a little
part-time delivering flowers for a floral company Valentine's Day
a few weeks teaching school at the Catholic High
(I told one class just wait'll you get out

into the real world and one kid
shouted THIS *is the real world
we're real students, these are real desks
this is a real school)*;

a part-time job installing satellite dishes
with a friend, taught a high school
religion class for kids
that went to public high
stayed home and began to learn to meditate
prayed a lot, read the Bible

started looking for work in social services
in all the big cities of our country.
We got a nibble from Cabrini-Green
in Chicago, corresponded with a Dorothy Day House
in Des Moines, talked to Good News
down in Florida and got an interview
in Omaha. We were hired to live-in
as house parents at a group home
for mentally handicapped men
and three and a half years later

Debbie was promoted, so we moved
into this house in a tough part of town
where people come by in their cars
and throw glass bottles to break on the sidewalk,
neighbors have screaming matches at 3 in the morning
some nights are filled with repeated gunfire.

Things got stolen off our porch
until we learned to keep it locked
so then they broke into the house twice
con men drifted by like we had
a neon sign in the front yard advertising for them,

we had garter snakes
get into the house the last two summers,
a bat flew into the house a few days ago,

(I was able to trap it in Mark's room
until the Humane Society guy
came by, put on his heavy leather
gloves, and caught the bat
just like a baseball
pitched to him from some other world,
took it out and I saw its weird
tiny face and heard it say *click click click*),

each winter mice invade
to eat their last suppers of my poison,
pigeons have come to roost on our roof
on the south side, maybe because
I started to feed the sparrows,

cockroaches have come back this summer
after the initial spraying 3 years ago
kept them all killed and away,
the ropes for the counter-weights
in the windows are breaking
one by one, the basement leaked
last summer in heavy rains,
continued to do so this summer, all our
books and papers and everything in storage got musty
and last summer my paintings
were covered with mildew,
which broke my spirit,

the Gulf War came and went
and it burned me back inside
like an old tree stump

and when Clinton went in, to bomb,
they showed that little Iraqi girl on TV
while the commentator blustered
about our strength and power
like a bunch of two-bit bullies,

I went into the bathroom and cried
you might say I was depressed
you might say that I gave up all hope
in politicians ever again, or governments
you might say that I gave up all hope
in humanity in general
and it was only moments before the TV thing
came on about the Iraqi girl
who looked so much like my Audrey
whom they showed her father crying over
and talked about how tough we are,

it was just before I read in a book
by Ralph Wiley how he was only
two blocks away from the motel
in Memphis, in his own home, when the word
of King's shooting swept over the city
like wildfire, then I saw the girl
then I went into the bathroom and wept
then I could not stop it anymore.

Debbie came to ask me if I was OK
and I said I was and explained
but I really wasn't, I was clinically depressed,
I was working three jobs and not doing well
in any of them, I was presiding over a volunteer
peace organization and getting wasted,
and the house was just recovering
from an invasion of fleas

we had to spray to kill three times
wash all our linen three times
spray poison in our cars
over and over,

so I quit everything but my main job
and the family, but the house
continued to fall apart
and after the drain for the tub
plugged up to not unplug
finally, after having slowed down
and plugged up enough times
that I had to snake it out
at least once a month
they came and knocked a hole
in the wall going up the steps
a hole about 3 feet long
by a foot-and-a-half high

and they cut out the rusted-shut pipe
and left the hole for our landlord
to repair, which they still haven't
and when the plumbers
were working on the pipes
they were getting electric shocks
off the ductwork, and they had to tear a hole
into the bathroom wall too
above the front of the tub

but the grout's all rotting in the tiles anyway
and the tiles are falling down
so we finally decided damn it
we're going to get ourselves a house
so we did even though we had bad credit
because we wrote the bank a letter

explaining what wonderful people we really are
so now the house is cluttered with boxes
filled with whatever we think is worth saving
for the rest of our lives.

3. Poem an Old Drunk Street Poet Told My Son

> "...I start thinking that, if I had not been born, another poor man could have drunk this coffee. I feel like a dirty thief..."
>
> César Vallejo
> "Our Daily Bread"
> trns. James Wright

Poem An Old Drunk Street Poet Told My Son At The Greyhound Station

There is an old dog
that lives in my house
and smells like the leather of my shoes

He sees the evil
the people who live there do
but he pisses on no one

Mailing Out Poems in Benson

The little girl
who lives down the street
two houses from the Benson P. O.
ran outside
and I heard her older brother's voice
scream at her
that she is a motherfucking son-of-a-bitch.

By the sound of his voice I would say he is ten or twelve
she looks to be about three.

She goes over to the side of the house
where there are some bicycles stacked
by the trash cans.

She doesn't do anything
stands without moving
head down, shoulders slumped
sings a little song.

One Saturday later
Mom and big Brother and little Sis
get into the family van
and she takes too much time
to get in the rusted sliding door,
and she can't get the sliding door shut.

Mom stomps around the van
from the driver's side
curses all the way
to slam the door so hard
it could have crushed the girl's arm in two
and I bet then in a poem

her arm would have broken off like a wing
and flown off to a better place
or fallen to the ground
which would be the ground of hell

but all that happened was that mom
stomped back around to the driver's side
slammed the car into gear
almost backed into an oncoming car
that had to swerve to avoid a collision,

and drove away.

Audrey

She's at the Baker's Supermarket, she says
walking in, when a young black girl
about ten, on a bike
spits at her.

She says *I smiled at her, Dad.*

I say *Next time*
instead of just smiling
try saying
hey how's it going
or something like that
when you first make eye
contact
language sometimes
breaks down barriers.

I tell her she fits the stereotyped image
of the dumb blonde
for some people
so she has to expect
to be treated
stereotypically.

She says
I just said the peace prayer
of St. Francis
over and over to myself,

and later in the car
my friends
wanted to make something of it

Looking for my daughter

disappeared around a corner behind
a stack of economy trash
bags and blue
jeans made by slaves

as if stepping into
a jungle path at Sam's
Wholesale Club a living
interactive monument
to our way

last flash
of her leg
heart catch

people stroll carts

fear in my eyes

can't they see

beautiful strange
language the muffled
chime-like intonations
of Vietnamese

Thoughts of the Encounter

Light still washes over the tree across the street
that belongs, if something like that can belong,
to my neighbor whom I have lived
a hundred feet away from for years
and have never met, except once, when I took around
the box for the Heart Association, and he slinked away,
as if he was afraid.

Briana's asleep now, has been
for a long time, before I realize
I'm staring at the movement of the tree
like a plant under the water,
and it is, of course, a plant under water,

and we are at the bottom of an ocean of air
where we swim around in our daily routines
oblivious to the waters we swim in.
An old cliché, isn't it?
It's an old cliché of city life

that one can live across the street from another
of his own kind and never learn
if the man of the house has red hair or black,
or if there are children there, or if
he believes in Jesus or Buddha or rocks and stars,
Democrats or Republicans or Nazis,

or if he thinks he owns that tree,
or if he has ever noticed it
or how the movement of its leaves
in the waves of a summer storm
of wind can hypnotize a man

who lives across the street from him.
I wonder if he has ever felt he had
such strange and amazing powers
through the grace of that one tree

or whether he knows what he would do
if I were to burst in his front door
now, suddenly, to embrace him
because he might be my brother—
before the night finally closes in on us.

The Candle

A man stands outside the house
holding a candle that burns
with a light bright enough he can see
where to walk,
but not bright enough
to see deeper
into the darkness. The light
in fact makes him less able to see
into the darkness,
lighting as it does
only the small globe
around the man himself,
blotting out all else
outside the globe,
because of the light's very brightness.

He could put out the light with his breath
or the wind could blow it out.
Either way, once his eyes
adjusted to the darkness he would see
better into it which does not explain
why the man felt the need
to light the candle in the first place
nor why it seems
he can't content himself
to live in darkness,
in which he sees so well.

The Museum of the Fur Trade, Chadron, Nebraska

High above us in the morning sun and air
two hawks tumble around each other,
then soar—
Is it a sign?
But I am no good at interpreting signs.

I stand in the parking lot to watch them
incise precise arcs out of my vision,
then back in, until they fly off south
into the pinewood forest.

I can't figure out the hawks.

Inside the museum, row
after row of carved wood and machined steel
devised by people who still
killed whales for spermaceti,
tortoises to make combs,
buffalo for their tongues,
and had not yet even invented the lightbulb—

many with their own inscription:

"... with this rolling-block rifle...,"
"...the .50 caliber Sharps rifle was...,"
"...with this .30-40 Krag, or one much like it, Colonel...,"
"...could propel a half-inch diameter ball of lead accurately nearly one
    mile...."

In the next room, beaded, almost whimsical clothing,
childrens' shoes with intricate beadwork,
rattles and ceremonial masks, stone-tipped arrows,
stone axes, buffalo bladder water bags.

Tomorrow At Seven

Sure as the executioner's clock,
my daughter will go to Bruegger's Bagel Bakery
for her first day of work
for pay, not counting babysitting.
She is only fifteen, won't be sixteen until October
and we are happy for her—
that her quality shone through
so much they are willing
to take a risk with her
one of only two under-sixteen-year-olds
the manager says, in the whole chain.

Still I can't help but feel a sense of loss
at this success, a loss for her
of her childhood, though she's eager
to work—a loss, too,
of a time in our world in which
children could be children until
they were eighteen or so, a blessed time
that happened, maybe, for only fifty years
or less, and happened
only in our country.

Maybe we were spoiled
this last generation, so many of us
growing up carefree teens,
living out the endless summers,
not needing to work, because our one parent
was able to bring home bacon
enough for everyone. Maybe it's just The Fall,
the continual re-creation of the fall out of bliss
into the ugly reality of life,
the fall in the garden that repeats itself

day after day in our world
where Cain's out killing Abel tonight again
just a few pages past the part
where everyone's running around naked
and don't even know it.

My Audrey will make a few bagels tomorrow
in the traditional way, boiled, then baked
as her ancestors did for centuries on end,
and she will have fun and smile at everyone
because that is what she does.
She will be good at her work
and she will not even notice, I don't think,
how stony the ground will suddenly have become
out there where the cars slide by like snakes on Dodge street,
where it's brother against brother, oh, my Audrey.

Skunk Beer

I went down to the store tonight to get a six-pack of beer
so that I could sit here at the table in my kitchen
and write poems and feel like a poet.
After I got the beer I stopped by the branch library
to drop some books in he depository that I decided
I will never read, though they were great things—
Calvino, Beckett, Heller, Borges,
funny poems by Sirowitz,
(I read the Sirowitz) then to the P.O.
to mail three poems to *Blue Violin*
whose editor had remarkably been nice to me in letters
although not taking any poems, and then back home,
cruising slowly down Maple
in no hurry, cop car circling the block.
Get home, tell Debbie I'm back, piss,
go get a beer, crack it, it's
Moosehead, my favorite, and the damn beer's skunked.

I remembered then something I had learned years ago:
never buy specialty beer at the neighborhood liquor store
where all the working-class stiffs go
to drink beer and shoot pool and fight,
go where the rich people buy their beer.

Tomorrow, when I wake up with a headache
I'll remember the other thing I learned
when I was seventeen and we slugged down those quarts
of skunky Pabst from our friend's car trunk
as we tried in that pitiful western Nebraska town
to dull the pain of whatever it was
each one of us knew needed to be dulled,
but could never explain.

Nap

I'm sitting on the blue La-Z-Boy in the TV room
waiting for Briana to fall asleep.
I watched Bob Ross teach how to paint landscapes a while,
now I'm reading contemporary short stories about demented people
who go around killing each other as obsessions,
and there are others addicted to living lives of shattered glass,
while she lies in her bed upstairs, reading Muppet Babies.

Something about a puff of cloud out in the northeastern sky
catches my eye—it's not a cloud
but the disc of the moon, barely visible.
She comes downstairs, declares she's not sleepy.
I know better, get her to lie down
first on one couch, then the other,
then finally she comes to me.
I put my book down and we rock.

I think of a painting I made yesterday,
lots of shapes of yellows, blues, greens and reds,
think how easy it would be for me
to learn to paint representationally—it is all technique
and refinement of technique. I try to see
shapes I draw up from inside, and color them in
and most all turn out looking like messes
which must mean that's what's inside of me,

but I decided sometime yesterday to stop
living and writing and thinking self-pity
and not to paint self-pity, and so I went to this piece
of cardboard, the flip side of Audrey's science display
and painted a bright picture of these shapes.
Briana, who had lured me downstairs to paint,
left me, went out with her mother to wash the cars.

They tried to trick me outside to spray me
but I stayed with the paint, and that was yesterday.

Now I feel her four-year-old body
on top of me, this body formed
out of my wife's body and of mine,
feel her lying on my chest like a curve
of the earth, feel her weight press me down
as she could not press down the earth
for she is but four, and I am a middle-aged man
gone to fat, with allergies, with self pity
for all the things in life I have never done.
Now I know for sure she is giving it up
because she relaxes against me and her breathing catches,
she turns sideways as we rock, her right arm
pulled weirdly behind herself
and I feel her small back under my hand as I pat it.
How many times too I have rocked her sister and brother!
Short jolts of electricity twitch through her arms and legs,
my eyes close and I see she is a green shape,
a huge translucent leaf with darker lines—
that she and I and our lives are the whole earth we are each made of.

It is only 4 AM

It is only the hour before sunrise.
It is only when the robins start to sing.
It is only the most beautiful sound that exists.
It is only air, moving through some other creatures' bodies.

Oh, Johnny, Oh!

We are laughing and falling over each other, going up the stairs to pat her to sleep, Briana and I, she who is seven, I who am 49, when the words to that old dance tune, a square dance, come to me—*and we all promenade with that sweet corner maid singing Oh! Johnny Oh! Johnny Oh!* and I am back outside the old basement house on Schafronick's quarter where the Farmers' Union meets, it is cold, a little snow flicks through the air, a shaft of light yellower than sunshine blasts into the night like a searchlight when someone bangs open the door down the dark steps where the dancers whirl.

On frozen ground, in the dark, my cousin and I snoop in the buttery squares of half-windows where the farmers and their wives, our mothers and fathers and neighbors, do-si-do to the directions of the caller. It is Nineteen Fifty-Seven, my brother has not been killed in his car wreck, our neighbor has not thrown himself on a hand grenade to save his Marine Corps buddies, nobody we know has been sprayed by anything called Agent Orange, nobody's ever heard of AIDS, *Oh! Johnny Oh! Johnny Oh!*

My cousin and I and all the dark light of the country look in on the dancers.

Ordinary Time

The last person involved in Wounded Knee—
soldier, prisoner,
in the bitter snow is dead,
no one living in this country
will be alive
born before rural electrification,

no one born before Enola Gay
came to Japan,
last guard or prisoner
from Nazi death camps, dead,

last person born before television
will be gone,
last born before every household
in the United States had a computer
will die,

last person from Desert Storm.
Sometime in there my wife
and I
will have died
not too many years
after that our children,
but people will go on inventing things,
destroying people.

Last person who on a hill had stood
far away from glare of city lights
looked at vast darkness,
wondered, saw clearly
the last time.

No one living
will know
who it was
the person
will not know
will die
an ordinary person among
ordinary persons
on just one more ordinary night to look up at the stars.

Cricket

I was up writing
and listening to Beethoven on the FM
Piano Concerto #1 in C Major
when I heard the cricket
in the TV room.
I thought I'd heard it this morning, too.
I got up and went out into the sunroom
and under cover of the third movement
was able to walk right up to the corner
where the cricket sat making its own music,
its way of looking for love.

Like a bat, I was able to home in
on the cricket first to discern for sure
it was not outside the open window,
then to locate its position
almost like you can pick out a certain player
in a symphony
though I could not see it
behind the long drapery.
I turned on the light and saw with my eyes
the cricket like a fat whole note,
small for such a robust sound.
I reached down,
expecting it to jump up as they do, into my palm
so I could carry it out
where all its cousins sang,
but it jumped away,
onto the cover of a *People* magazine
lying crumpled there beside it.

I picked up the magazine,
carried it outside into the many songs of night

and shook it gently.
I never saw it fall, since it was dark,
so I flipped through a few pages,
shook it gently again,
still saw no cricket,
but thought it must be out.
I could hear Beethoven
shimmering in the background
and on the porch,
over by the open bedroom windows,
where my wife lay sleeping,
another cricket called.

I came back in and saw on the cover
Jennifer Aniston's breast
partly exposed, leafed through the pages
to look for the cricket
in the dim foyer,
past pages of faces,
fingers magnified
to the size of sausages, landscapes
of actor's faces and chests,
huge actresses legs,
parts of breasts,
closeups of womens' faces.

Sacrifice

The last time I saw Mike Iron Shield
was at the American Indian Center
in Alliance, Nebraska. You know,
it's been almost twenty years since I saw him,
and I can't remember anything he said,
exactly, I just remember
he was always funny.
He was an alcoholic
and didn't worry about it.
It was the life he knew,
and he did it well—
sleeping in the park,
eating out of the trash.
Only problem was,
how to get his daily wine.

Today a friend said he'd died,
victim of rotted meat
he'd fished out of the Dumpster
behind Safeway.
Died of the flesh
of what the Lakota called "spotted buffalo"
when first they saw them,
refused them as rations
because they couldn't believe
anyone would eat something
that smelled so bad.

Died of that,
rather than the Thunderbird
he changed each day
into his own body and blood.

Peanut Butter

Just back from a walk,
dripping sweat on the wooden floor.
Briana's on the couch.
It's a hot night, she can't get to sleep.
Debbie's finishing up some dishes
since she can't read in the TV room
in the recliner because the light
keeps Briana awake.

I pat her a bit. No good.
I'm irritable, toss the couch pillows
onto the floor with a *pop!*
when she flips one of them over
onto my sweaty body.
I can't believe
how angry I get
these days over petty stuff.
She fusses around, can't get comfortable.
In my leaden state
I finally realize it's the heat,
ask her if the fan's getting to her.
"Hardly," she says.

I find an extension cord,
plug it in, get the fan closer to her.
"Ah, Daddy, that's wonderful," she says.
I talk to Debbie in the kitchen,
two or three minutes later Briana's asleep.
I put in some laundry, clean the bathroom floor,
come to the kitchen
to do this hot and cold water therapy
for my eye, hoping it will heal faster.

This is one of my few quiet times to think.
Going to work every day I hardly get a chance.
All I can think about is getting the kids
where they have to go, getting ready
for work, going to work, running errands,
being at work, coming back from work.
Weekends I barely recover,
Sunday nights, start thinking
about work again.

This is what happens—
two mornings ago
I didn't even notice
when Briana sat with me at the table
with two slabs of toast,
a jar of Super Crunch Skippy
and a knife, and smeared
peanut butter all over the bread—
the miracle of that.

Cricket Redux

Every time I find a cricket in the house I put my hand around it, and it jumps around trying to get away but as soon as it's in my hand it becomes still, as though it trusts me, it seems comfortable in my hand. I carry it to the door to outside and when I open up my hand the cricket does not want to get off. It is content to stay there in my hand. I think I am the St. Francis of Assisi of Crickets. I like their little brownish black bodies like a pair of worn-out old shoes, and their funny little antennae that stick out all over the place like little cop cars or mobile army command units. I like it that they like me enough to stay in my hand. I would start a traveling circus for crickets but I don't think that I'd make enough money at it to support my family and then my wife and I would argue over it and she would leave me. She would take the kids, and then I wouldn't see them again except on weekends when I came to visit. I would be so weak by then from sorrow any one of them, even the youngest, would have to pick me up off the floor and carry me outside like a cricket in her hand. I am not cute and black and I don't have any antennae. I would sit in a room all day hidden in some corner but I wouldn't be able to rub my hands or legs together to make music. I would be no good as a cricket. So I guess will not start a cricket circus. Besides, it would be demeaning to the crickets to have to wear little suits or to be hitched onto tiny wagons. I don't think that a cricket would do that. They have more self-respect than that, I bet. I bet you can't even find a cricket that will pull a wagon anymore. You can just find the ones that sing all night. They are a bunch of great singers, those crickets, they are one great song, one great song of the earth, one great song about something you can hold that will seem to like you and forgive you. Gentle Reader, you could go downstairs right now, and find a cricket, and pick it up, and carry it in your hand.

The Microwave

At work one day last week the microwave quit. Lots of us did not believe it, we all had to come in and make our official tests: mine was green tea that came out cold; somebody else tested old pizza. Diagnosis the same. Then the ones who thought it might just be a fuse or loose wire had their try—the screws came out, the side lifted up like somebody's ribs when they open your chest—the fuse was fine, and nobody could even find a wire. Diagnosis still the same, our course of action determined. One of us went around to collect five dollars from each user, just like we do when somebody's family member dies. An ad hoc committee was formed, decisions made on the place with the best deal, price range, features, color.

The new one arrived in its cardboard egg. The white came out and the part we saved, the gray-black electronic yolk, came out to rest on the freshly scrubbed counter, which no one had realized till then had not been cleaned in maybe seven years. I picked up the old one and someone said since I held it in my arms I may as well take it to the Dumpster the contractors have on the lawn frozen into the spring snow. Somebody had checked and it's OK, we can throw stuff into their Dumpster.

So I heaved it and it made a perfect curve in the air in the bright morning sun and landed without a noise among the discarded two-by-fours, broken wallboard, old carpet, shattered pieces of trim—this old microwave that heated everyone's food for what was it . . . was it six, or seven years? No one could remember for sure.

Front Page Story in the *Omaha World-Herald*

This fella named Ricketts
bought a house
at 412 Elmwood Drive
which might not have been
that big a story
except that he paid
seven point five million

well, shoot, it was completely
remodeled,
11,000 square feet on 4 acres,
movie theater in the basement
tennis court, swimming pool
6-car garage
"Not a bad view
out any window,"
the real estate guys gushed

seems this fella Ricketts
owns 63% of American Trading
which he's taken
twenty-three years
to build up to where
he's got it

he says
my wife and I've got
four children to raise

the article spilled over
to page two
and the real estate guy gushed some more

"This puts Omaha right up there
with Kansas City and Chicago!
We're not the poor sister
in the housing market any longer."

A little to the left
below where
the article
ended

a one-half-inch filler

about the Chief of the Quinault tribe
"the last of the Elders,"
"deeply respected"

dead at eighty-one
from a self-inflicted gunshot wound

Doing Laundry

Sort through pieces of cloth designed blessed
by touch woven by some people I do not know
sewn by still others most for slave
wages for others whose only desire
only love
is money

things many times over blessed product
of minds which spent time to design
them each piece different sized proportioned
to fit all the different shapes each one of us
has blessed because someone sweat
in fields and buildings once or maybe now
worked by slaves to grow cotton
run machines spin rayon acetate nylon spandex

blessed because hands wove fibers into fabrics
controlled machines rolling bolts of cloth inspected
with intelligent eyes and fingers blessed
because hands loaded fabric into boxes onto pallets into trucks
drove forklifts into cavernous trailers blessed because

truck drivers wove fabric
through dark behind lights because fingers
ran machines day-in day-out for little
or no pay sewed fabrics into shapes of human
parts placed pieces on racks
shoved racks down passageways to hands
to sort by size kind color blessed
by hands packing them into cardboard
cartons other hands broke
open unpacked tagged hung on racks shelved rang
through registers blessed this piece of cloth shaped

by someone's hands into cups
for breasts cloth these for feet
arms legs torsos someone's

hands pressed against flesh
of my family hands we will never
know many now dead touched
our bodies passed blessings
to us

see
this little violet sock my child had
her foot in its sole coated
impregnated browned blessed
with earth it has come from see
this blessed sock protected
my daughter's foot someone's hand
held her foot

with other pieces of fabric I wash
it in the plastic and metal machine made
by still other workers
the mechanism once again kicks in
power wired here from
ancient plants pulls pieces
of fabric shaped like parts of our bodies
deep into water blessed
water holy water from which
they came to mingle wash
together with soap sweat dirt
and mistakes of all the ages

To The Citizens of Omaha, Nebraska

Now it is five in the morning.
The first robin has begun to sing.
There is no reason for you to drive your cars
past my house at this time of the night.
Why aren't you home in your beds sleeping?
Why aren't you home writing poems?
Making love? Writing novels? Why aren't you home?
Why do you have to drive past my windows,
which I have open tonight, July 11th, 1999
because it is a really wonderfully cool night?
What do I have to do to convince you?
Here comes a car that's barely running.
I can hear it hitting on about 4 out of 6 cylinders.
What will they do if the car breaks down
at five o'clock in the morning?
Citizens of Omaha, go home. Take a rest.
I have been up all night writing poems.
You can go home and relax.
I have been here to hear the first birds sing.
What a joyous sound it is.
It does not need your car noises added to it.
The robins' song is perfect as it is.
You are probably too drunk to know.
You think you are having some kind of life.
I am telling you: go home.
Get out of your God-forsaken cars.
Get your book of lined paper.
Write down the words the birds tell you to write.
See if that makes some difference in your lives.
The birds say go home.
Get out of your cars.
Sing.

This Morning

I come out into the kitchen in early morning
turn on the water to let it run one minute
to get the water cleared of dissolved metals.
Out the window two robins hopping around.
It is just before the official start of spring.
Their being here tilts this earth a little closer toward spring.
They may not know that, or they may.
But what difference could that possibly make?
Who knows if they are aware of what they do?
They come here every spring, whether they think about it or not.
They have been coming here and landing here on this spot of hill
that eventually became my backyard
since long before time was invented.
Before spring was given a name, by anyone.
They do not know I am in this house
looking out the window at them
another day in which I will go to work
and they will not.
Another day that my wife is leaning over the tub
washing her hair, and our oldest daughter
has already driven herself off to school.
Another day our youngest child will sit
once more at this table to eat cold cereal
and read her *Archie* comics.
That the robins would read too
if they were she, perfect as they are.
She and I and the birds and her mother,
we have always been coming to this morning.

What I Like

is when the lights are out in the house and I'm heading off to bed in
my sock feet and I step on one of the boards in the floor and it gives

a little. What I like is when I get a letter from somebody and can
tell the person who sent it to me is a smoker because the envelope

and the letter smell like stale smoke. What I like is to get some
honey on my fingers, just a little bit, and not know it and get

it on something else like a knife handle or a doorknob, and then have
to try and figure out all the places I got honeyed up. And what I

like is to run some warm water on a white dishrag and go around
and wipe all the honey off all the things I got the honey on. And what

I like too is to open a new book and put it up to my face and flip
the pages to smell the ink and paper smell come out of the book.

And I like to check a book out of a library and find a cigarette
ash in it or a crumb of something or a piece of snot. Maybe

you are the one who left it there. I like to know that
there are others living here, doing the same things I am doing.

I like to be in traffic, maybe right behind your truck,
and smell the tinny stench of your exhaust. I like to know

you are on your way, and that I am following along behind
or maybe even am headed on my way too. I like to know that

people are headed on their ways, even if they don't know where they
are going. I like to be part of that. Even though it makes me

almost blow chunks, I like to smell your bad breath because
you are alive, and you are talking to me. Oh sure, I like

to smell the hyacinths in the grocery store
somebody broke off that hang there like,

well, broken hyacinths.
What I like is that even someone's destructive urge

or some dumb accident
can't stop us from knowing we are alive.

ABOUT THE AUTHOR

Greg Kosmicki's poems have been published in numerous literary periodicals. He is the author of six chapbooks and two previous books of poetry. He was awarded Artist's Fellowships from the Nebraska Arts Council in 2001 and 2006. Greg is the editor and publisher of The Backwaters Press. He and his wife Debbie live in Omaha and are the parents of three children.

www.ingramcontent.com/pod-product-compliance
Lightning Source LLC
Chambersburg PA
CBHW071145090426
42736CB00012B/2238